Editing Scientific and Medical Research Articles

Dr Claire Bacon

First published in the UK in 2021 by
Chartered Institute of Editing and Proofreading
Apsley House
176 Upper Richmond Road
London
SW15 2SH

ciep.uk

Copyright © 2021 Chartered Institute of Editing and Proofreading

ISBN 978 1 915141 08 8 (print)
ISBN 978 1 915141 09 5 (PDF ebook)

All rights reserved. No part of this publication may be reproduced or used in any manner without written permission from the publisher, except for quoting brief passages in a review.

The moral rights of the author have been asserted.

The information in this work is accurate and current at the time of publication to the best of the author's and publisher's knowledge, but it has been written as a short summary or introduction only. Readers are advised to take further steps to ensure the correctness, sufficiency or completeness of this information for their own purposes.

Development editing, copyediting and proofreading by CIEP members Liz Dalby, Margaret Hunter, Abi Saffrey, Cathy Tingle, Sonia Cutler, Bev Sykes.

Typeset in-house
Original design by Ave Design (**avedesignstudio.com**)
Creative commons images from Unsplash and Pixabay [and/or credits]

Contents

1 |	Introduction	1
	The purpose of this guide	1
	Why do scientists need editors?	2
	The focus of this guide	3
2 |	How to edit a research paper: Suggested workflow	4
	Creating the brief	4
	Suggested workflow	6
3 |	Structure of a research paper: What the editor should look out for	9
	Abstract	10
	Introduction	11
	Methods	13
	Results	16
	Discussion	17
4 |	Editing tables and figures	19
	Tables	19
	Figures	24
5 |	How to tackle common issues with scientific writing	26
	Poor readability	26
	Troublesome words/common confusables	33

	Biased language	36
	Plagiarism	39
	Tenses in research writing	40
6 |	Scientific style	44
	Scientific terminology	44
	Nomenclature	46
	Numbers and units	47
	Capitalisation	49
	Abbreviations	50
7 |	Helping with the publication process	52
	Pre-submission enquiries	52
	Cover letters	53
	Rebuttal letters	54
8 |	Resources	55
	CIEP	55
	Scientific style guides	55
	Non-scientific guides	56
	General information on scholarly publishing	56
	Books on scientific writing	57
	Books on author editing	57
	Plain English guides	57
	Dehumanisation in clinical practice	58
	Other useful resources	58

1 | Introduction

The purpose of this guide

This guide is for editors who want to work directly with scientists, helping them to write research articles that are clear and easy to read. The purpose of this guide is to explain:

- how to edit a scientific paper (with a suggested workflow)
- the overall structure of a research paper (Abstract, Introduction, Methods, Results and Discussion) and possible structural problems the editor should look out for
- how tables and figures should be edited
- common issues with scientific writing and how to fix them
- points of scientific style
- how to help clients navigate the academic publication process (pre-submission enquiries and cover and rebuttal letters).

Why do scientists need editors?

The purpose of this guide is to give editors the tools and information they need to edit scientific research papers. Why is this necessary?

Scientific research articles must be clear and easy to read to make sure that the reported findings are properly interpreted and implemented. Although these findings can be complex, it is often the writing rather than the science that makes scientific articles difficult to understand. There are different reasons for this.

Many scientists struggle to write clear, readable sentences in English. Others forget who they should be writing for: the reader. They believe that scientific writing *should* be complicated and difficult to understand – a misconception that they can inherit from their supervisors. Skilled editors who understand how to structure a research paper and how to write readable sentences can help make sure the author's intended meaning is clearly communicated to their peers and the public.

Scientific language editing is in great demand. According to the fifth edition of the International Association of Scientific, Technical and Medical Publishers report, over 3 million articles were published in 2018 and this number is growing. In addition, scientists are under pressure to publish. Without publications, they cannot win grants to fund their research or secure permanent positions. Authors who find it hard to write clearly in English are at a disadvantage here. Language editors can level the playing field by making sure that these scientists communicate their valuable findings effectively to the scientific community.

The focus of this guide

This guide focuses on getting a research paper ready for publication in a scientific journal, either before or after the article is submitted to a journal. When the article is submitted, the journal Editor decides whether the paper is suited to the scope of the journal or not and either rejects it or sends it on for peer review. A paper that is well written and properly structured has a much better chance of being sent for peer review. This is the goal of editing at the pre-submission stage. Papers that have been accepted for publication are probably already well structured. At this post-submission stage, the editor needs to make sure that the language and style are clear and consistent. The principles described in this guide will be useful to editors working at both stages.

What is involved in editing a scientific research paper? This varies greatly from paper to paper and usually depends on how much writing experience the author has. If the author has written a paper before, then copyediting to improve readability and ensure consistency will probably help. If the author has limited writing experience, they may benefit from developmental editing that considers the overall structure and coherence of their text. This guide provides the information you need to edit research papers on both levels.

2 | How to edit a research paper: Suggested workflow

Creating the brief

Editors usually follow the brief given to them by the client. However, scientists will probably not provide a detailed brief and style guide when they hire you for an editing job. Some are not aware of the differences between developmental editing, copyediting, and proofreading, and do not know what a style guide is. They are more likely to ask you for 'a language polish', 'a quick proofread' or 'a language check'. Use your knowledge and experience of editing to assess the manuscript and create a brief based on your client's needs. Be sure to explain to your client what type of editing you think the manuscript needs and what you can do to help. Taking the time to do this will increase awareness of what editors do and will make your future professional relationship with this client much easier. If the client wishes to proceed, then you can agree on a brief, deadline and fee together.

The following is a suggested workflow for editing a scientific research paper at the pre-submission stage. (Editors working on post-submission papers should receive a brief from the journal's editorial team.) This workflow will vary depending on the paper and the brief you have agreed with the client. The client may have a limited budget and ask you to focus on selected issues to save time and money. A balance between what you think is adequate editing and what the client can afford can be difficult to negotiate. If it helps, give your client a list of things that were not included in your brief and advise them to check these before

submitting their paper to the journal. For example, you can edit the text for readability and consistency and then recommend that they check that the data in the figures and tables match that in the text. The author may also ask you to ignore their references – possibly because they have used reference manager software or because they do not have the budget to pay for this. In these cases, you can recommend that they make sure the reference list is complete (all in-text citations included in the reference list and vice versa) and that the formatting is consistent.

It can help to do another pass after the client has reviewed your changes, particularly if you have suggested structural changes or if the level of editing is heavy (for example, if many sentences have been rewritten to improve readability). Make sure the client knows whether this additional pass is included in the original fee or not.

Suggested workflow

1. **Check the journal's instructions for authors**. These can be found on the journal's website. Journals usually provide detailed instructions on formatting but rarely provide detailed instructions on English usage (possibly because the journal copyeditor will make sure that the article meets the style requirements once the paper is accepted for publication). If this is the case, follow the main style guide used in the field and make sure the style is consistent (see chapter 8 for common style guides used in the different scientific fields). It may not be necessary to make changes if the author has used a consistent style and the journal has not stated that this is incorrect.
2. **Check that the author list is complete**. (Are all authors in the author list mentioned in the Author Contributions section and vice versa?) Has an affiliation been given for every author?
3. **If you use PerfectIt, run it to catch inconsistencies**. (This is particularly useful for catching inconsistent or unnecessary abbreviations.) You can also customise PerfectIt to match a particular style. Paul Beverley's FRedit macro can also make multiple style changes at once. These options are useful if you edit many papers for one journal.
4. **First pass: check for overall coherence**. Do the Introduction, Methods, Results and Discussion sections contain the relevant information? This is explained in detail in chapter 3, but here is an overview of what you should check for:
   a. *Abstract*: does the Abstract include the rationale, research question, methods, main results and conclusions? Have the implications been discussed?
   b. *Introduction*: has the author described the knowledge gap the study will address, the background information needed to understand the study, the research question and a description of how the research question will be answered?
   c. *Methods*: has the author described all the procedures and materials used? Can the reader replicate the experiments and analyses with the information provided? Is the information clearly structured so that the reader can find what they are looking for?
   d. *Results*: are the findings presented in a logical order? Are the data

presented relevant to the research question or would they serve the reader better in the supplementary information? Are the results described in an objective manner (no interpretations or conclusions)? Are all the data from this study?
   e. *Discussion*: has the author repeated and answered their research question in the opening paragraph? Is there any unnecessary repetition of introductory information or results? Is all the literature relevant to the research question? Have the strengths and limitations of the study been discussed? Has the author emphasised the overall implications of their work?
5. **Second pass: edit for readability**, adding comments to explain any heavy editing, such as why a sentence has been completely rewritten. Are the sentences clear and easy to read? Tips on improving readability are discussed in detail in chapter 5, but here is an overview of what to check for:
   a. Has the active voice been used where appropriate?
   b. Are the subject and verb close together?
   c. Has the author used strong verbs?
   d. Are parallel constructions used in lists and when making comparisons?
   e. Are the sentences concise? Are any unnecessary wordy phrases present?
   f. Do abbreviations help the reader or should full definitions be used?
6. **Check the figures**. This is discussed in detail in chapter 4, but in brief you can check for the following:
   a. Are the results clearly presented and easy to interpret?
   b. Have all figures been referred to in the text and in the right order?
   c. Do the data presented in the figures match the descriptions in the main text?
   d. Does the information in the figure legend match the figure?
   e. Are all symbols, shading or abbreviations explained?
   f. Is the figure legend complete and clear?
   g. Does the figure contain any data that are already described in detail in the text?
   h. Is the style consistent between figures?
   i. Are all units of measure provided?

7. **Check the tables.** This is explained in more detail in chapter 4, but here is an overview of what to check for:
   a. Are the results clearly presented and easy to interpret?
   b. Have all tables been referred to in the main text and in the right order?
   c. Do the data presented in the tables match the main text?
   d. Are percentages calculated correctly? Are the ranges correct?
   e. Are all symbols explained in the legend/footnotes and in the right order?
   f. Does the information in the table legend match the table?
   g. Does the table contain any data that are already described in detail in the text?
   h. Does the title describe what is shown without interpreting the results?
   i. Are all rows and columns properly labelled (with units)?
8. **Cross-check the data in the Abstract**: do they match the main text and figures/tables?
9. **Cross-check the data in the Results**: do they match the Abstract and figures/tables?
10. **Edit the references.** Are all the references in the list cited in the main text and vice versa? Is the referencing style consistent and correct? Has the author included the digital object identifier (DOI) for journal references if the journal requires it?
11. **Final proofreading pass to catch any remaining errors.** You may wish to leave this stage until later when the client has had a chance to review your edits and return the paper to you. In this case, make sure the client knows whether this final pass is included in the agreed fee.

3 | Structure of a research paper: What the editor should look out for

Original research papers are typically organised into the following sections. It is beyond the scope of this section to describe the references in detail; please refer to chapter 1.8 of the European Association of Science Editors (EASE) *Science Editors' Handbook* for an excellent guide on this topic:

- Abstract
- Introduction
- Methods
- Results
- Discussion.

This organisation helps the reader find specific information quickly and easily. For example, if they want to know how an experiment was conducted, they look in the Methods section; if they want a summary of the main findings, they look at the beginning of the Discussion. Unfortunately, scientists sometimes fail to structure their papers according to this convention and thus their paper lacks coherence. The purpose of this chapter is to explain what information should go into each section and highlight common issues to watch out for.

Abstract
What should be included?

The Abstract summarises the rationale, approach, results and conclusions of the work. It is the only part of the article (along with the title and author list) that readers see when searching electronic literature databases and may well be the only part they will read as some full-text articles are only available on a subscription basis. This means the Abstract must describe the work as a whole. To do this, it should include the following information:

- the rationale (why the study was performed)
- the research question (what was studied)
- the methods (how the study was performed)
- the main findings/conclusions (what was shown)
- the implications.

Most journals impose a limit of around 250 words on the Abstract, so it needs to be clear and concise to include all these points. Covering each point in two or three sentences at the most will help meet this word limit. The journal will specify whether the Abstract should be structured (divided using subheadings) or unstructured (written as a continuous paragraph).

What the editor should look out for

Although writing two or three sentences about each of these points seems like a simple task, many authors do not cover all the points and often focus too much on one point. For example, they will write six sentences of introductory information and finish with a sentence or two about the main findings. Or they will describe the results without emphasising the rationale or the research question. Authors often do not realise this when they read through their Abstract since they can easily infer the missing information – an editor can help here.

Check that the background information is concise and, most importantly, relevant to the research question. The author should explain why their study is important and what gap in the knowledge it will fill within the first few sentences. Consider adding a comment if they have not. Also note that citations should be avoided in the Abstract.

Next, the author should tell the reader what they are going to do to address this problem/knowledge gap. This is the research question around which the entire study is centred so it needs to be clearly described. If you are not sure what the research question is after reading the Abstract, consider suggesting that the author make this clearer.

The methodology and results should properly address and answer the research question. Authors often have so many results that they fail to describe the most relevant results in their Abstract. For example, if the research question is whether a novel anticancer drug increases overall survival and the author only reports symptom scores, then a comment would help, such as:

> Your main research question is to investigate overall survival after drug administration but here you report only the symptom scores. Please consider describing the data on overall survival in the Abstract so that your main research question is answered.

Introduction
What should be included?
The Introduction gives the reader the information they need to understand what was done and why. It should:

- explain the problem/knowledge gap the study will address
- give the information needed to understand the study
- state the specific research question
- describe how the research question was answered.

What the editor should look out for
The focus of the Introduction develops from general information to the specific research question. The author should start by telling the reader why the research is important. This is usually done by presenting the context and background and then highlighting the problem or knowledge gap. Scientists can lose focus in their writing, so check that the information in these opening sentences relates to the study aims and research question. For example, if the author is investigating a novel

treatment for lung cancer but talks about why novel treatments for breast cancer are needed, then consider adding a query, such as:

> These opening sentences should explain why your study is important. To do this, please make sure the information presented in the Introduction is related to your specific study aims and research question. In the Introduction, you highlight the lack of effective treatments for breast cancer but the drug under investigation targets lung cancer. It would be more helpful to describe the current situation regarding lung cancer treatment. This will tell the reader why this new drug is needed.

The next few paragraphs tell the reader what they need to know to understand what was done and why. Ideally, the author should start by describing the current state of knowledge and narrow this down to the specific gap in the knowledge that the research question will address. This information should be concise and relevant to the research question – consider raising a query with the author if the information does not seem relevant.

After the background information comes the research question. This should address the gap in the knowledge that was described, be specific and be within the scope of the study. Vague statements that go beyond the scope of what is being investigated lack credibility. For example, a suitable research question would be:

> In this study, we investigated whether drug X affects one-year overall survival in a UK patient cohort.

A vague and less credible question would be:

> In this study, we investigated whether drug X can reduce lung cancer mortality.

Methods
What should be included?
The Methods section explains how the study was conducted. This information allows the reader to judge the results and repeat the experiments. The Methods section includes the following information:

- study design
- what was studied (such as animal model, human participants, cells)
- what was done (interventions and experimental procedures)
- what was used (equipment and materials with the manufacturers' details)
- what was measured (outcome measures)
- how the data were collected and analysed.

Each of these points is described in more detail below.

Study design
For clinical trials, the type of trial (such as parallel, crossover, factorial) should be given. If a new drug is being tested, the trial phase (I–IV) should be specified. For studies using animal models, the groups being compared should be described (for example, wild-type mice versus genetically modified mice).

The author should also describe how they randomised animals or human participants to each group and whether researchers were blinded to group allocation throughout the study. This allows the reader to judge whether the reported outcome effects are overestimated.

Animals and human participants
In animal studies, authors should describe the species, strain, sex, weight and age of the animals. In trials with human participants, providing the eligibility criteria used to select the participants tells the reader whether the findings are relevant to their own clinical practice. Authors should also specify how participants were recruited and whether informed consent was obtained. If the need for informed consent was waived, this should be made clear.

Studies involving animals and human participants usually require ethical approval and the author needs to state who granted ethical approval for their study and give the approval number.

The author needs to explain how they calculated the sample size, which power calculation they used and the primary outcome this calculation was based on. This information is important because it indicates the probability that the study will find a clinically or scientifically important difference. In animal studies, it also shows that no more animals than necessary have been used.

Interventions or experimental procedures

In a clinical trial, the interventions for each group should be described, including any control interventions. In studies using animal models, the model should be described together with the methods used to measure the outcomes. Details on animal care and handling should also be provided because these can affect the results.

Equipment and materials

All materials and reagents used in the study need to be clearly identified and the source provided. Chemicals and biological materials should be described using standard nomenclature (discussed in chapter 6) to avoid ambiguity. The model number and manufacturer of any specialised equipment should also be given.

Outcome measures

An outcome measure is a variable that measures the effects of a specific intervention. Studies often have several outcome measures, which are categorised as primary or secondary outcomes. The primary outcome is the most important and is used to calculate the sample size. Secondary outcomes are less important but are still relevant to evaluate the effect of the intervention. The primary and secondary outcomes should be clearly defined, with details on how and when they were evaluated.

Statistical analysis

The statistical methods used for each experiment should be described so that the reader can evaluate the appropriateness of the analysis and whether the conclusions are valid. The author should include the outcome measures, independent variables and tests they used. They should also explain how they handled any missing data and how they adjusted for multiple comparisons. The software used for the analysis together with the version/release of each software package should also be described.

What the editor should look out for

It is not the editor's responsibility to make sure that all the relevant methodological information described above has been included. However, if you notice that something is missing, such as ethical approval to work with animals or informed consent from human participants, then consider adding a query for the author. Sometimes an author will describe the results of an experiment without explaining how the experiment was performed. Be sure to add a comment if you notice this. Also check whether the author has included the manufacturers' details for the equipment and reagents used.

Check that the information has been clearly structured so that the reader can find the information they are looking for: has the author divided the Methods section into subsections with appropriate subheadings? (There are no rules on what order this information should be presented in, but the study design is typically described first and data analysis is typically described last.)

Results
What should be included?
The purpose of the Results section is to present the findings in a clear, objective and logical manner. This is typically done using:

- Narrative text: this guides the author through the results, explaining what the main findings were. Simple relationships among data and concise quantitative information can also be presented as text.
- Figures: these can be used to present complicated relationships among qualitative data or to show patterns and trends among quantitative data (usually in the form of graphs). They can also be used to present visual data, such as images, photographs or diagrams.
- Tables: these are useful for presenting large amounts of quantitative information, particularly if the reader needs to be able to make multiple comparisons between different items.

The structure of the Results section will depend on the study design and the journal guidelines. Reporting guidelines are a useful resource for structuring the Results section because they provide a checklist of important information needed for the reader to understand and use the results (see chapter 8 for more information on these guidelines). Different study designs each have their own guidelines. For example, the Consolidated Standards of Reporting Trials (CONSORT) checklist for clinical trials suggests seven subsections for the Results section (participant flow, recruitment, baseline data, numbers analysed, outcomes and estimation, ancillary analyses and harms).

What the editor should look out for
Check that the author has divided the results section into logical subsections with relevant subheadings. For example, the results could be ordered to match the research question and hypotheses that were outlined in the Introduction or the experiments that were described in the Methods. The most relevant results (for example, the primary outcome in a clinical trial) should be presented first followed by the secondary findings.

To maintain focus, data that are not relevant to the research question should be put into the supplementary information. Although it is not the editor's responsibility to decide whether data are relevant or not, if you find that some figures and tables distract you from the main message of the paper, then consider bringing this to the author's attention and suggest they use the supplementary information.

The author should remain objective and should not interpret the data or draw conclusions. Look out for words like *caused*, *suggesting* and *indicating* here and consider adding a comment if the author has interpreted the data. Also check that the author only describes data from their own study in the Results section. Any comparisons with published findings should be saved for the Discussion – this includes the author's own published data.

Check that the author has been as specific as possible when describing their results. Flag vague statements that add no value to the narrative, such as *The overall survival rate was different between the two groups*. How was it different? Which group had the higher survival rate? Consider adding a comment for the author, encouraging them to be more specific.

Please refer to chapter 4 for a more detailed discussion of editing tables and figures.

Discussion

What should be included?

The Discussion is the final section of a research paper. The purpose is to conclude the research story by answering the research question and explaining what the results mean. Unlike the Introduction section, where the author describes general information and then gradually focuses on the specific research question, the Discussion should describe the specific findings before moving on to the broader implications. In short, the Discussion should:

- repeat the research question and then answer the research question based on the presented results
- discuss the presented results in relation to the published literature
- explain the strengths and limitations of the study
- specify the conclusions and broader implications of the work.

What the editor should look out for

Many scientists make the mistake of starting their Discussion by reintroducing the topic. Make sure that the author repeats their research question and answers this question with a summary of their main findings in the opening paragraph. If they have not, consider adding a comment, such as:

> The Discussion should start by reminding the reader of the research question and then answering this question with a summary of the main findings. This will remind your reader what the study is about and will prepare them for your analysis and interpretation.

Make sure that the author does not continue to repeat background information and that they focus on presenting their results and discussing these in relation to the published literature. Consider adding a comment for the author if they repeat information from the Introduction:

> The purpose of the Discussion is to discuss the implications of your findings in relation to the published literature. Please avoid detailed repetition of introductory information and focus on discussing your results.

Also watch out for detailed repetition of the results. While the author can remind the reader of trends and relationships, they should not provide too many specific numbers with P values.

Check that the author discusses the strengths and limitations of their work in the penultimate paragraph before the conclusions. Some authors are reluctant to emphasise the weaknesses of their study, but it strengthens the integrity of the paper. If a discussion of the limitations is missing, consider adding a comment for the author, such as:

> Please discuss the limitations of your work before drawing your main conclusions. This will show the reader (and the peer reviewer) that you have considered the potential weaknesses of your work and will strengthen the integrity of your research.

4 | Editing tables and figures

Tables and figures are useful tools in a research paper because they allow large amounts of complicated data to be presented in a clear and simple way. Figures are useful for presenting complex relationships in qualitative information whereas tables are better suited to displaying exact values in quantitative information.

Tables

The purpose of a table is to present detailed quantitative information in a clear and simple way so that the reader can find relevant information quickly and easily. To do this, the table needs to be properly constructed. There is no universal design, but tables typically contain some or all of the following components:

- table number and title
- column headings
- column spanners (additional column headings that identify the contents of two or more columns)
- table spanners (additional headings that cover the width of the table to divide the data)
- stub (the left-hand column that contains the row headings)
- data field (the main body of the table)
- table footnote.

These components are illustrated in table 1.

Table 1 The key components of a table

Table number	Title					
	Table spanner					
Stub	Column spanner			Column spanner		
	Column heading	Column heading	Column heading	Column heading	Column heading	Column heading
			Data field			
Footnotes:						

Most journals will have a style guide for tables – make sure the author has followed these instructions.

What the editor should look out for

Tables are referred to in the main text

All tables (including supplementary tables) must be referred to in the relevant place in the main text and in consecutive order. A quick search for 'Table' in the text is a good way to check this. If a table is not mentioned in the text, add a comment for the author:

> Please note that all tables must be referred to in the main text in consecutive order. Table X is not mentioned in the main text. Please refer to this table in the text or reconsider whether it needs to be included.

Make sure the author has referred to the tables by their number rather than their position in the text, which may change in the final typeset version (*see Table 1* is better than *see the table below*). Standard style is to capitalise *Table* when referring to a specific table (that is, *Table 1 shows* not *table 1 shows*).

Data in the tables are not repeated in the main text

Data from tables should not be repeated in detail in the text. The author should focus on the relationships between variables in the narrative so the reader can see how the results address the research question. Watch out for sentences that repeat specific values and suggest modifications to put the data into context. For example, *Overall survival was significantly higher in group A than in group B* is a better sentence in the main text than *Overall survival was 68% in group A and 43% in group B (P < 0.01; Table 1)*, which just repeats what is shown in the table.

Data are accurate and consistent with the data presented in the main text

Errors are common in tables, particularly in large tables presenting lots of data, so it is important to carefully check the values in every data field. Here are some specific things to look for:

- Have the values been correctly identified? (For example, if a column header identifies the values as percentages, make sure that every data field in that column contains a percentage value.)
- Are all percentage values and total values correct? (A quick search for '%' will identify all percentage calculations for checking.) Any discrepancies, such as those due to rounding up, should be explained in the footnotes or legend. Are the numerator and denominators provided? (This is important for the reader to interpret the data – there is a big difference between 2/4 and 5,000/10,000 but both are 50%.)
- Are ranges correct? (Look for overlapping figures in the ranges, such as ≤30, 30–40, 40–50.)
- Is the level of precision appropriate for the measurement? For example, height and percentages are usually best presented at the integer level (*183 cm* is better than *183.45 cm* and *63%* is better than *63.45%*).
- Are the values presented in the table consistent with those presented in the Results or Abstract?

Each table is focused on one topic and makes a clear point

Rather like a paragraph in the main text, a table should deal with one topic and present one main idea. Check that the reader can understand the main message of each table without reference to the main text. If the point of a table is not clear to you from the title, data and table legend then add a comment for the author with suggestions for improvement.

Title briefly describes what the table shows and does not interpret the results

To help a table stand alone from the main text, it should have a short but descriptive title that tells the reader what it shows. Check that the title does not provide detailed background information (such as the different categories presented in the column headings) and that it does not interpret the results (for example, *Overall mortality in lung cancer patients receiving either drug X or placebo* is a better title than *Overall mortality is higher in lung cancer patients receiving drug X*) – the reader should be allowed to draw their own conclusions by reviewing the data.

Column headings are brief but informative

Different categories of information should be presented in separate columns in the table and each column heading should tell the reader what the data in that column show without going into unnecessary detail. If the author has repeated information in the column headings, consider suggesting spanner headings to avoid unnecessary repetition, such as *Type of surgery* to avoid having to repeat *surgery* in the column headings.

Table footnotes are consistent with the information in the table

Table footnotes provide additional relevant information that would otherwise overcrowd the table, such as definitions for abbreviations and notes on a specific row, column or cell that are annotated in the table with symbols or superscript letters. Check that any abbreviations or symbols defined in the footnotes are present in the table and that they are defined in the order that they appear in the table. For example, asterisks are often used to indicate P values in tables (*P = ≤0.05, **P = ≤0.01, ***P = ≤0.001).

Tables have a clear layout

There are no set rules on how to organise information in tables, but the reader will understand the data better if they are presented logically and clearly. If a table is overcrowded, suggest adding white lines (if space restrictions allow it) to promote clarity. Boldface type should be used sparingly in tables and should not be used to indicate significant values – a superscript symbol (usually an asterisk) with an explanation in the legend is a better way to do this.

To promote a clear layout, make sure that all the content is relevant to the main message and that no information is repeated, either within the table or from other tables. Also look out for redundant information, such as identical elements in a whole column – for example, if all patients received drug X, then a column entitled *Type of drug* is redundant. A note to this effect (*All patients received drug X*) in the footnote would be better. Putting units in every data field can be another source of unnecessary clutter – suggest giving the units in the column/row headings or footnotes.

Check that the data are arranged in a way that conveys the message clearly. For example, if a table is presenting mortality rates in patients with different tumour types, mortality rates can be presented from lowest to highest so that the reader can easily see which tumours have the highest mortality rates. Otherwise, tumour types can be listed alphabetically, so that the reader can quickly find the mortality rate for patients with a specific tumour type.

Figures

Figures serve different functions in a research paper, from summarising data and illustrating complicated patterns to describing how an experiment was conducted. Figures can promote the readability of a research article by clarifying complicated concepts and giving the eye a break from blocks of text. Readers may look at the figures to quickly determine what the paper is showing. Therefore, figures need to be clear, they need to tell their own story and they need to stand alone from the main text. How can the editor make sure that the figures in a research paper are fit for purpose? Let us consider what you should look for.

What the editor should look out for

Figures are numbered consecutively in the text

The reader needs to understand the significance of the figure and how it contributes to the research story; this needs to be explained in the narrative. Check that every figure has been mentioned in the relevant place in the text and that the figures are numbered consecutively.

The information in figures matches that in the text

Authors sometimes change the figures during the writing process and may forget to adapt the text accordingly. Therefore, it is worth checking that each figure shows what the author says it shows in the text. Also make sure that data in the figure match what is written in the Results and Abstract.

Data from the text are not duplicated in the figures

Make sure that each figure tells its own story rather than simply duplicating data already described in the text. For example, a figure may illustrate the relationships between multiple variables.

Figures are well presented and consistent

Figures need to contain all the relevant information to understand the main point and they must be easy to interpret. Look at each figure and see whether you can quickly ascertain what it is showing. If not, consider raising this issue with the author.

For a more specific evaluation of the presentation, check whether the following criteria are met:

- the text is minimal and easy to read
- the figure makes optimal use of space with no unnecessary white space
- all shading, symbols and abbreviations are defined or explained in the legend
- any use of colour is necessary (keeping in mind that information may be lost if the reader prints the article in black and white)
- in graphs, the x and y axes go beyond the range of the highest values so that all data are included
- style is consistent between figures (same font, font size, symbols, abbreviations, numbering system) and the author has followed the journal guidelines
- the units of measure are provided
- highlighting (such as bold or italics) to add emphasis is minimal and necessary.

The figure legend is complete and clear

Check that all figure panels are included and explained in the legend. Also make sure that all symbols, shading, colours and abbreviations are defined in the legend (if they are not already defined in a key). The figure title should describe what the figure shows but should not specify the type of figure, such as *Bar chart showing* ... If the figure has been reproduced, make sure the author states that permission has been obtained to reproduce the figure and gives credit to the copyright holder.

5 | How to tackle common issues with scientific writing

Poor readability

Plain English is important in science. Unfortunately, scientific writing is often difficult to understand – and the writing rather than the science is usually to blame. This section tackles the main reasons for poor readability and suggests ways to make scientific research articles clear and easy to understand.

Use the active voice where appropriate

Sentences written in the active voice are often more concise and easier to understand than passive constructions (*24 participants completed the questionnaire* is shorter than *The questionnaire was completed by 24 participants*). Search for *by* to identify passive constructions that could be changed to more readable active constructions.

Your client might be reluctant to use the active voice, particularly if it involves using first-person pronouns, probably because they have been taught that the active voice should be avoided and that scientific writing should be completely objective. Remind them that this opinion is outdated – most high-impact journals now advocate using the active voice to improve readability and using the first person can strengthen the conviction of their arguments and ideas, if used sparingly. Encourage your reluctant clients to browse published articles in top journals; they will see that the active voice and first-person pronouns are often used.

Note that the first person is most effective in the Discussion section when presenting counter arguments (*In contrast to the opinions of Smith et al.,* ***we*** *believe that ...*) and showing conviction in a main result (***We*** *showed that a trusting patient–clinician relationship is key for discussing non-physical symptoms*). The first person is less useful in the Results section, where data need to be described objectively (*Regular exercise reduced stress in healthy individuals* is better in the Results section than *We discovered that regular exercise reduces stress in healthy individuals*).

But edit passive constructions with care. It is not always appropriate to change passive constructions to active ones in scientific writing, especially when the reader is more interested in what was done rather than who did it. This is particularly relevant in the Methods section where protocols are described: *Cells were cultured at 37°C in a humidified incubator* is more suitable in the Methods section than *We cultured cells at 37°C in a humidified incubator*.

Changing passive constructions to active ones may also disrupt the focus in a sentence. Consider the following example:

> The theory of special relativity was developed by Einstein.

Before you change this to *Einstein developed the theory of special relativity*, consider what the author wants to say. If the main topic of their sentence is special relativity and not the life and works of Einstein, the passive voice will improve readability by getting straight to the point. Also, if the previous sentence ended on the topic of special relativity, then the author may wish to start their next sentence with this known information before presenting new information (that Einstein developed the theory), so the passive voice better serves their purpose. This approach of presenting known information before new information is a useful strategy for writing clearly, particularly in scientific articles where the author is presenting complicated information and ideas.

Keep the subject and verb close together

Scientists often separate the subject from the verb with intervening information, making their sentences harder to understand. This can also lead to subject-verb disagreement because it is no longer clear what the subject is. For example:

> **Non-small cell lung cancer**, which includes adenocarcinoma, squamous cell carcinoma and large-cell undifferentiated carcinoma, **account for** nearly 9 out of 10 lung cancer cases.

The point of this sentence is that non-small cell lung cancer is the most common type of lung cancer. However, separating the subject (non-small cell lung cancer) from the verb (accounts for) has led to subject-verb disagreement (*account for* instead of *accounts for*). The sentence would be clearer if we kept the subject close to the verb and put the intervening information into another sentence:

> Non-small cell lung cancer (NSCLC) accounts for nearly 9 out of 10 lung cancer cases. The three main types of NSCLC are adenocarcinoma, squamous cell carcinoma and large-cell undifferentiated carcinoma.

Intervening information enclosed within parentheses can also lead to subject-verb disagreement if the author does not know that parenthesised information should not influence the choice of verb. For example, in the following sentence:

> Non-small cell lung cancer (adenocarcinomas, squamous cell carcinomas and large-cell undifferentiated carcinomas) **account** for nearly nine out of ten lung cancer cases.

The verb *account* does not agree with its singular subject (*non-small cell lung cancer*). Changing the verb to *accounts* so that it agrees with its singular subject will help the reader understand the sentence.

Conjunctions that do not make the subjects they join plural (for example, *or* and *as well as*) and singular pronouns that are often mistaken for plural (such as *each* and *every*) often cause subject-verb disagreement in

research writing because authors think they should use a plural verb. For example, in the following sentence:

> Each of the participants **were** asked to complete the questionnaire before the study started.

The verb *were* does not agree with the singular subject (*each of the participants*). Changing the verb to *was* improves clarity.

The phrase *the number of* also often leads to subject-verb disagreement because the writer thinks the verb should agree with what comes after *of* rather than *number* (which is singular). For example, in the following sentence:

> The increasing number of minor alleles were linked to more severe depression in female participants.

The verb *were* does not agree with its singular subject (*number*). Changing the verb to *was* shows the reader that we are talking about the number of alleles and not the alleles themselves.

Use strong verbs

Scientific writing often contains empty verbs that add no information to the text. Common culprits include *performed, caused, provided, resulted, observed* and *showed*. Using a stronger verb introduces action to the sentence and makes the sentence more readable. For example:

> Drug use correlated negatively with overall mortality in patients with lung cancer

is much clearer than

> We observed a negative correlation between drug use and overall mortality in patients with lung cancer.

Note that changing the weak verb (*observed*) to a strong verb (*correlated*) avoids the need for nominalisation (*correlation*) and makes the sentence easier to read.

Use compound nouns instead of prepositional phrases

Prepositional phrases (such as *rate of patient survival*) consist of an object (*patient survival*) and a modifier (*rate*) joined by a preposition (*of*). Removing the preposition and using a compound noun (*patient survival rate*), where *rate* directly modifies *patient survival* is often easier to read, particularly in longer sentences. But keep in mind that it is not always appropriate to change a prepositional phrase to a compound noun if doing so would interfere with parallelism, for example (more on this next).

Use parallel constructions

Parallel constructions consist of grammatically equal elements and can make long, complicated sentences much easier to understand. This is particularly relevant in scientific articles when authors present and compare complex information.

Parallelism is particularly helpful in lists. Consider the following example:

> The goal of this study is to understand how amyloid-promoting factors contribute to age-related amyloid diseases using three main approaches:
>
> - investigating how amyloid-promoting factors interact with amyloidogenic proteins
> - to identify proteins that interact with amyloid-promoting factors
> - how do these interaction proteins regulate amyloidogenesis?

This list is not easy to understand because, in addition to containing complex words, the three items in the list are not grammatically equal. The first starts with a gerund (*investigating*), the second starts with an infinitive (*to identify*) and the third is phrased as a question. So, what should the editor do? There are three possible solutions: start all three with a gerund, start all three with an infinitive or phrase all three as a question. The latter option is not ideal because the second element cannot be easily phrased as a question. You could either start each element with a gerund (*investigating how amyloid-promoting factors interact with amyloidogenic proteins, identifying proteins that interact with amyloid-promoting factors* and *determining how these interaction proteins regulate amyloidogenesis*) or start each element with an infinitive (*to investigate how amyloid-promoting factors interact with amyloidogenic proteins, to identify proteins that interact with amyloid-promoting factors* and *to determine how these interaction proteins regulate amyloidogenesis*).

Parallelism is also helpful when comparing variables. Making sure that every variable being compared has a similar grammatical structure and uses similar words will help the reader to see how they are connected. For example:

> Chemotherapy was more effective than administering immune checkpoint inhibitors at reducing tumour size.

In this comparison, a noun (*chemotherapy*) is being compared with a participle phrase (*administering immune checkpoint inhibitors*). Changing the second variable to a noun helps the reader to understand the connection:

> Chemotherapy was more effective than immune checkpoint inhibitors at reducing tumour size.

We could improve the parallelism even further by changing *immune checkpoint inhibitors* to *immunotherapy*, which is more similar to *chemotherapy*. However, check with the author to make sure their intended meaning is retained. (They may want to emphasise that immune checkpoint inhibitors rather than another type of immunotherapy were used.)

When checking for parallelism, remember that parallel constructions are sometimes deliberately avoided to make a sentence more concise. For example:

> Eleven patients fully recovered, 8 needed another operation, 4 required occupational therapy and 1 died in hospital.

Here, repeating *patients* after each number makes the sentence more cumbersome to read. The missing information is implied in the sentence and excluding it improves readability.

Use fewer words

Replacing wordy phrases with more concise alternatives can improve readability. For example:

Changed **instead of** *resulted in a change in*
Explained **instead of** *accounted for the fact that*
Because **instead of** *due to the fact that*
Can **instead of** *have the ability to*

Removing any redundant words, such as *past* history, few *in number*, large *in size*, round *in shape*, *very* significant, *very* unique and *pregnant* parturients (the redundant words are italicised) can also make the text easier to read. Also keep an eye out for unnecessary repetition, for example:

We recorded the type of abdominal surgery (open abdominal surgery vs laparoscopic abdominal surgery)

can be shortened to:

We recorded the type of abdominal surgery (open vs laparoscopic).

Using affirmatives instead of negatives can also reduce the number of words; for example, *reject* instead of *do not accept*, *different* instead of *not the same*, *prevent* instead of *do not allow* and *insignificant* instead of *not significant*.

Troublesome words/common confusables

There are many words that are often misused in scientific articles. Here are some common culprits to watch out for.

Compose and comprise

Compose means to make up and comprise means including or containing. A common issue in scientific articles is using *comprised of* instead of *composed of*. For example, changing The treatment approach was **comprised of** surgery and chemotherapy to either The treatment approach was **composed of** surgery and chemotherapy or The treatment approach **comprised** surgery and chemotherapy will improve the accuracy of the text.

Continual and continuous

Continual means to recur at frequent intervals and continuous means to go on without interruption. Add a query if you think the author may have confused these terms; for example, if they refer to a *continuous intravenous infusion for three days* make sure they realise that this means the patient was infused without interruption for three days.

Dose and dosage

Dose refers to the amount of a drug given at one time (*A 40-mg dose was administered every hour*) and dosage refers to the amount and frequency of administration, usually expressed as a quantity per unit of time (*The dosage was 40 mg per hour*).

Fewer and less

Fewer is used with countable items and less is used with non-countable items. For example, change *There were less patients in the treatment group* to *There were fewer patients in the treatment group*. Authors also mix up *amount* and *number* – make sure they use amount when referring to non-countable nouns and number when referring to countable nouns (*A higher number of patients* not *A larger amount of patients*).

Risk and harm

A risk is the chance that something hazardous can cause harm. Risk is often used incorrectly to mean harm in research papers. For example, the sentence *There is a risk of radiation exposure during a CT scan* is rather misleading. There is no risk of radiation exposure here – the patient will definitely be exposed to radiation if they have a CT scan. The author probably means to talk about the risk of harm after radiation exposure.

Respectively

Respectively indicates a one-to-one correspondence between two or more items. In the Results section, it is typically used to make lists of data more concise (*The mean age of participants in group A, B and C was 56, 45 and 49 years, respectively*). The problem with *respectively* is that readers will often need to reread the whole sentence to grasp the meaning. Check whether *respectively* really helps the reader and consider recasting the sentence if the author has only listed a few values (*The mean age was*

56 years in group A, 45 years in group B and 49 years in group C; here, the reader will not need to read the sentence twice to figure out which mean age belongs to which group).

Another common issue when using *respectively* is not specifying what the values refer to. For example:

> The mortality rates were 24% and 40%, respectively (Table 1).

You can improve this sentence by adding the missing information (you may need to ask the author for clarification here):

> The mortality rates were 24% and 40% in male and female patients, respectively.

The values need to match the descriptions when using *respectively*. Consider the following example:

> The mortality rates were 24%, 40% and 38% in male and female patients, respectively.

Here, the author presents three values and two descriptions, which will confuse the reader. Ask the author to clarify what the final value refers to.

Endemic

This describes a disease that is constantly present in a particular population or region. A common inaccuracy is using *endemic* to describe a region, for example, *Parts of Africa are endemic for malaria*. Make sure the author uses *endemic* to describe the disease (*Malaria is endemic in parts of Africa*).

Negative and positive, abnormal and normal

These words are often used to describe a test when they should be used to describe the test result. For example, *The coronavirus test was negative* should be changed to *The coronavirus test result was negative*. The same is true for abnormal and normal: *The brain scan was normal* should be changed to *The brain scan results were normal*.

Acute and chronic

These describe the duration of symptoms, conditions or diseases (acute = short term, chronic = long term) but are sometimes incorrectly used to describe severity. Another mistake is to use acute and chronic to describe patients, treatments or medication. For example, *The patient received chronic treatment* should be changed to *The patient received long-term treatment* or *The patient received treatment for their chronic condition*.

Significant

This term should only be used to describe differences between variables that have been proven to be statistically significant using an appropriate test. The relevant *P* value should be provided in parentheses. Also look out for phrases like 'almost significant' and 'a trend towards significance'. Many scientific style guides do not accept these phrases because differences are either significant or not significant – there is no in-between.

Biased language

Scientific articles, particularly health-related research articles, often include information about human participants. Biased language that categorises people based on their sex, race or ethnicity, age, disabilities or sexual orientation is usually offensive and inaccurate and should be brought to the author's attention.

Look out for any irrelevant information about the study participants. The participants' sex, race or ethnicity, age, disabilities or sexual orientation should only be mentioned if it is scientifically or medically relevant to the research question.

Gender and sex

The terms sex and gender should not be used interchangeably according to scientific style guides. Sex refers to the biological differences between males and females whereas gender indicates a person's personal identity. Make sure the author has used gender-neutral language, such as singular *they* rather than *she* or *he* as a gender-neutral pronoun. This will also avoid excluding trans and non-binary research participants who do not identify as male or female.

In clinical studies, it is often necessary to specify how many participants were male and how many were female because the biological differences between the sexes can affect the findings. Make sure the author has used *male* and *female* as adjectives rather than nouns to avoid dehumanising the participants (*there were 43 female participants* instead of *there were 43 females*). Sex is still largely considered to be binary in the scientific and medical literature, so specific guidelines on how to refer to non-binary individuals in research writing is still lacking. This may change in the future as research uncovers the biological and clinical relevance of non-binary sex on disease pathology and treatment.

Race and ethnicity

If the author has defined the racial or ethnic origins of their study participants, make sure they have explained why. Encourage the author to be as specific as possible when referring to racial and ethnic groups. Asian American, for example, is vague – ask the author if they can specify where the participant's ancestral origins are. Specific words to describe groups should also be favoured over generalisations such as *racial minorities*. Race is often avoided in journals because it is a rather narrow concept, grouping humans according to shared physical traits. These physical traits are now understood as largely a result of adaptation to different geographies and climates. There is no genetic basis for race: in fact, there is far more genetic variation within so-called races than between them. Ethnicity or ancestry is preferred because it is based on the broader cultural expression and place of origin.

Disabilities and disease

Before we talk about the language of disabilities and disease in scientific writing, it is important to acknowledge that there is no universal agreement on which terms are suitable, even among members of the relevant communities. For more guidance on this, please see the CIEP fact sheet on disability terminology for writers and editors (see chapter 8).

The language the author uses to describe people with disabilities should respect their integrity as human beings. Point out problematic phrases such as *confined to a wheelchair* (inaccurate because wheelchairs are not prisons, they allow their user to move freely). Encourage people-first language when the author refers to people with a disability or disorder (*people with diabetes* is more acceptable and less dehumanising than *diabetics*). However, in health-related research papers where people with diseases or disabilities are referred to many times, some journals accept the adjectival form (*cancer patient* instead of *person living with cancer*) to improve the readability of the text. Some communities do not prefer people-first language. For example, some people with autism prefer to be referred to as *autistic* because they are proud of their neurodiversity. However, the journal may have a different perspective and insist on people-first language.

The author should not use terms that suggest helplessness when talking about people with disabilities and diseases (such as *victims*, *afflicted*, *maimed* and *sufferers*). Negative descriptions of conditions should also be avoided. For example:

- Use *intellectual disability* not *mental retardation*.
- Use *substance use disorder* not *substance abuse problem*.
- Use *brain injury* not *brain damage*.
- Use *physically disabled* not *crippled* or *deformed*.

Referring to study participants

Make sure the author refers to their study participants in a respectful way. A common issue is referring to *cases* instead of *patients*: a case is an occurrence of a disorder or illness and a patient is a person affected by a disorder or illness who is receiving treatment. Phrases like *Schizophrenic cases were treated with antipsychotic medication* are not appropriate; *Patients with schizophrenia were treated with antipsychotic medication* is acceptable. Also make sure the author does not refer to the patient when they mean to refer to the treatment – patients are not managed according to their symptoms, treatment is managed according to the patient's symptoms.

Language is more respectful if participants are cast as the subject (those acting) rather than the object (those acted upon), for example, *Participants completed the questionnaire* is better (and clearer) than *We administered the questionnaire to participants for completion.* In addition, most journals and medical style guides now ask authors not to refer to their study participants as *subjects* – *individuals* or *participants* is more appropriate.

It is important to educate healthcare professionals on how to avoid dehumanising language, but it is also important to remember that these people deal with tragic and stressful situations on a daily basis. Using dehumanising language to describe patients is likely the result of unconscious emotional detachment, a protective mechanism that allows them to do their job, rather than a disrespect for their patients. Support your clients by pointing these issues out gently and with understanding.

Plagiarism

Plagiarism is presenting somebody else's ideas as your own. In research writing, most cases of plagiarism are caused by insufficient acknowledgement (not crediting the original author for their ideas). Some scientists deliberately plagiarise because of the extreme pressure they are under to publish their work. Others may plagiarise accidentally,

particularly if they struggle to write well; for example, they may use a published article as a template for their own paper.

Whether plagiarism is deliberate or accidental, the consequences of it are severe, so query anything that you suspect might be plagiarised. This could be a sudden change in style (such as from UK to US spelling or from one referencing style to another) or a sudden improvement in the readability of the text. If your client plagiarises, help them to avoid this in the future by encouraging them to plan the overall structure of their paper before they start writing. The templates outlined in chapter 3 will help here. This will distinguish between their own ideas and those that need a citation. Also encourage them to keep notes on the key messages in the articles they cite. This will help them to remember where they got their information from.

Tenses in research writing

Tenses are important in research writing because they explain the time framework of the research story. The main tenses used in research writing are the simple past, simple present and present perfect.

The simple present tense

The simple present tense is used to describe established facts that probably will not change. In a research paper, the simple present can be used:

- in the Introduction to describe known facts, for example:

    Lung cancer is the leading cause of cancer-related death worldwide.

- in the Introduction and Abstract to state the study aims/research question:

    In this study, we investigate the effect of a novel anticancer drug on overall survival in patients with lung cancer.

- in the Discussion, to describe what the study has shown:

    In this paper, we show that drug X significantly increases overall survival in patients with lung cancer.

- to emphasise that a published finding is still valid and relevant:

    This remains the best-studied treatment for lung cancer.

- to refer to tables and figures when describing the results:

    Table 1 **shows** the patient characteristics at recruitment.

The present perfect tense

The present perfect tense is used to stress the present importance of a past event. In a research paper, it can be used:

- to emphasise the relevance of a cited study to the own work:

    Immunotherapy **has been shown** to increase one-year survival in people with lung cancer.
    (Here, use of the present perfect to describe a published study on immunotherapy in lung cancer emphasises that this topic is relevant to the research question in the present study.)

- to connect what is known with whatever gap in the current knowledge the study will address:

    Although immunotherapy **has been linked** to improved survival in lung cancer patients, very few immunotherapy drugs have been tested.

- to describe what the results show (like the simple present):

    In this study, **we have shown** that drug X significantly increases overall survival in people with lung cancer.

The simple past tense

This tense is used to refer to a completed action. In a research paper, it can be used:

- to describe the methods and findings:

    Overall survival **was** recorded.
    Overall survival **was** higher in the treatment group.

- to report published findings from a specific study:

    Bloggs et al. **described** how to culture cortical neurons from mouse embryonic tissue.

Things to watch out for

Using the present perfect correctly

Scientists sometimes use the past tense to describe things that are relevant to the present or relevant to their study. Using the present perfect can clarify the meaning in these cases. For example:

> Immunotherapy was widely implemented to treat lung cancer

can be changed to:

> Immunotherapy has been widely implemented to treat lung cancer

to emphasise that immunotherapy is still used today or if the author is testing an immunotherapy drug in their study.

Multilingual scientists sometimes overuse the present perfect tense – probably because they are translating directly from their own language. In German, for example, the present perfect tense is often used for normal past tense statements. But in English, if the statement is not relevant to the present, the simple past tense should be used instead.

Switching tenses

Another common issue in research writing is switching tenses while discussing one topic at a particular point in time. Sentences like this often crop up:

> Although postoperative complications **decreased** in the experimental group, the five-year mortality **increases**.

In this sentence, using both the simple past and the simple present to describe results that were found at the same time confuses the reader. The simple present (increases) needs to be changed to the simple past (increased) for clarity.

Use of continuous tenses

Continuous tenses are used to indicate that something is ongoing, which is usually not needed in a scientific research paper. The experiments have already been performed and the results are presented – nothing is ongoing. Continuous tenses should be avoided because they clutter the text with unnecessary use of the verb *to be*. The past simple is more concise and easier to read (for example, *We measured creatinine levels* is easier to read than *We were measuring creatinine levels*).

6 | Scientific style

Consistent style is important in scientific research papers because variations in the use of nomenclature, numerals and capitalisation may confuse and distract the reader. This chapter discusses the following elements of scientific style:

- terminology
- nomenclature
- numbers and units
- capitalisation
- abbreviations.

Your first port of call for all things style-related is the journal's guidelines for authors, where the style points you should follow are outlined. If these guidelines do not answer your style questions, you can refer to one of the many style guides for scientific writing (see chapter 8 for a list of style guides for different scientific fields). Some style conventions differ between these guides; common sense and good editorial judgement can ensure clarity and consistency. The purpose of this chapter is to emphasise common conventions in scientific texts and give tips on dealing with scientific style.

Scientific terminology

Scientific terminology is often complex and is constantly evolving. Even an editor with years of research experience will not understand every word of every paper they edit. As with every project, you should be prepared to do some research when you come across terminology you do not understand. Google Scholar is useful for checking the meaning of words and phrases and articles in the reference list may provide useful background information on the topic.

Do not worry if, after checking Google and asking around, you still do not understand something. Remember that your job is to serve the reader and not every reader will be an expert. If you do not understand something, there is a good chance the reader will not either and it is helpful to let the author know that additional explanation may be needed.

Sometimes, complex terminology can make it difficult to diagnose the problems in a sentence. A useful trick is to replace these words with letters, as shown below.

Step 1: highlight the complex terminology:

> Polydimethylsiloxane (PDMS) is currently one of the key materials used in microfluidic chips used for mammalian cell applications. PDMS microfluidic chips are constructed using the soft lithography technique where the formation of microfluidic channels is done by moulding of the prepolymer on a master and subsequent curing in an oven.

Step 2: replace this terminology with letters:

> A is currently one of the key materials used in B used for mammalian cell applications. C are constructed using the D technique where the formation of E is done by moulding of the prepolymer on a master and subsequent curing in an oven.

Step 3: now it is much easier to spot readability issues and the text can be edited:

> Polydimethylsiloxane (PDMS) is a key material of microfluidic chips for mammalian cell applications. PDMS microfluidic chips can be made using soft lithography. The microfluidic channels are formed by moulding the prepolymer on a master before curing in an oven.

Compound words (where prefixes or suffixes are added to a base word) are common in scientific writing. Generally, closed-up forms are preferred to hyphenated forms, including compound words with the following prefixes (although some journals using UK English such as *Nature* prefer hyphenated terms):

- non (nonsignificant)
- multi (multicentre)
- post (postoperative)
- co (coexpression)
- sub (subcategory)
- extra (extracellular)
- re (reoperate).

Exceptions include words that could be misunderstood (such as re-cover/recover), words where the prefix and base word end and start with the same vowel (such as co-operate) and words where the base word is capitalised or abbreviated (such as sub-Saharan).

Nomenclature

Naming things in a consistent way is essential for clarity in research writing. Scientific knowledge is continuously progressing, with new molecules, drugs, genes, species and so on being discovered every day. Without established systems of naming things, this information could not be usefully exchanged. Most scientific disciplines have special committees to develop these systems.

Keeping track of changing nomenclature is impossible. (The 11th Edition of the *AMA Manual of Style: A Guide for Authors and Editors*, for example, has more than 270 pages dedicated to nomenclature – and this is just for medical literature.) Be prepared to constantly refer to style guides or online resources for up-to-date guidance on scientific nomenclature. If you come across unusual nomenclature while editing a research paper that is not in the style guide, bear in mind that your author may be using a state-of-the-art term. Add a polite query suggesting that the author explains that this is new up-to-date usage.

Numbers and units

Numbers

The convention in scientific writing has been to use numerals for numbers 10 and above and words for numbers below 10. However, some style guides (including *Scientific Style and Format: The CSE Manual for Authors, Editors, and Publishers* and the *AMA Manual of Style: A Guide for Authors and Editors*) have highlighted that using numerals in some instances and words in others may be jarring to the reader and that digits convey quantity more effectively than words do (*a 3-mg dose* is better than *a three-milligram dose*). These style guides recommend using digits to express numbers, with some exceptions. Words should be used instead of numbers in the following circumstances:

- numbers at the start of a sentence (if possible, recast the sentence to avoid this)
- if two numbers are adjacent to each other, for example, *two 5-mg doses were administered* (words should not precede abbreviated forms of units, so *2 five-mg* doses would be incorrect here)
- when *one* and *zero* are not connected to a unit of measure or are not linked to other numbers, for example, *zero tolerance* but *between 0 and 6 weeks*
- in idiomatic phrases, such as *a day or two* or *a thing or two* (these phrases tend to be unspecific and redundant, so consider rewording them)
- common fractions, such as one-third or one-half
- ordinals from first to ninth.

Scientific notation

Very large and very small numbers should be expressed as powers of 10 in scientific writing (for example, 5.6×10^4 instead of 56,000 and 5.6×10^8 instead of 560,000,000). In ranges, both limits of the range should be written out in full (for example, 5.6×10^4 to 8.2×10^4 instead of 5.6 to 8.2×10^4).

Scientific notation does not need to be used if the numbers are not experimental quantities. For example, *We included 13,600 patients from 43 trials in our systematic review* is easier to read than *We included 1.36×10^4 patients from 43 trials in our systematic review*.

Scientific units

Research articles use SI units (from Système International d'Unités or International System of Units). These include seven base units and an unlimited number of derived units. The base units are:

- m (metre) for length
- kg (kilogram) for mass
- s (second) for time
- A (ampere) for electric current
- K (kelvin) for thermodynamic temperature
- mol (mole) for the amount of a substance
- cd (candela) for luminous intensity.

Derived units include units that have been given their own names, for example:

- °C (degree Celsius)
- Hz (hertz)
- J (joule)
- N (newton)
- V (volt)
- W (watt).

Other derived units are named according to the base unit, such as:

- m^2 (square metre) for area
- m/s (metres per second) for speed
- m^3/s (cubic metres per second) for volumetric flow.

A more complete guide to these derived SI units can be found in chapter 12.2.1 of *Scientific Style and Format* and chapter 1.4 of the *EASE Science Editors' Handbook* (see chapter 8).

Ratios, proportions and percentages

The values used to calculate percentages should be presented with the percentage so the reader can interpret the results. For example, *We collected blood samples from 40% of patients* is not very informative – *We collected blood samples from 42/106 (40%) patients* is better.

Ratios are presented as two numbers separated by a colon and not as a single number (for example, *The ratio of male to female participants was 1:4* not *The ratio of male to female participants was 4*).

Capitalisation

In scientific texts, capitalise the following:

- taxonomic names of a kingdom, phylum, class, family, order and genus but not the specific epithet in the species name (*Homo sapiens* not *Homo Sapiens*) and not the plural or adjectival form (*Streptococcus* but *streptococci*/*streptococcal*)
- in common names of organisms that include a proper noun (such as the Japanese Beetle) and sometimes in common names to avoid confusion between an adjective describing a common name and the common name itself (*White Heron* rather than *white heron*)
- brand names, such as *Plexiglas*
- proper names used as adjectives, such as *Fermi–Dirac statistics*
- official names of equipment, such as the *Large Hadron Collider* particle collider or the *Cosmic Background Imager* telescope
- the complete titles and subscales of medical tests (except for the word 'test', unless it is part of the name), such as *Personality Assessment Inventory* and *Mini-Mental State Examination* (shortened versions of the test name, such as *personality test* or *mental state exam* should not be capitalised)
- figure and table names when referring to them in the main text (that is, *Figure 1 shows* not *figure 1 shows*)
- in gene and protein symbols, capitalisation should be styled according to species: for human gene and protein names, all letters are capitalised (*FOXP1 gene*, *FOXP1 protein*); for mouse gene and protein names, only the first letter is capitalised (*Foxp1 gene*, *Foxp1 protein*).

In scientific texts, do not capitalise:

- words from which an acronym is derived (*enzyme-linked immunosorbent assay* not *Enzyme-Linked Immunosorbent Assay* for *ELISA*)
- letters within a word to show how a study name has been derived, for example, *PREventive Effect of FENestration on Post-Kidney Transplantation Lymphatic Complications (PREFEN study)*
- names of conditions or groups in an experiment, for example, *The mortality rate was higher in group A* not *The mortality rate was higher in Group A*.

Abbreviations

Abbreviations are more helpful to the reader if they are used sparingly in scientific writing. If you find yourself struggling to keep track of what your client's abbreviations mean, then add a comment for them to reconsider the number of abbreviations they have used. Journals do not usually set limits on the number of abbreviations allowed, but the author should only use them to improve readability and not to reduce work. Some journals help by specifying in their guidelines how often a term should be used in the text to justify an abbreviation.

Many scientific words are better known by their abbreviations and can be used without definition, such as deoxyribonucleic acid (DNA) and polymerase chain reaction (PCR). Non-standard abbreviations (abbreviations that are not widely known and accepted) should be defined when they are first used. This is usually done by spelling out the term in full and then giving the abbreviated form in parentheses directly after.

If you come across an undefined abbreviation, check whether it is recognised in the main literature database of the field (a quick check in Google Scholar should help you find a relevant database). This will tell you whether it is a standard abbreviation or not. For example, for medical and life science articles, check the Medical Subject Headings (MeSH) browser of the National Library of Medicine (**meshb.nlm.nih.gov/search**). Also check the journal guidelines – some journals provide a list of accepted abbreviations in their instructions for authors. These may include subject-specific abbreviations that are well established in the journal's field. For example, *Diabetologia* accepts GTT (glucose tolerance test) and HOMA (homeostatic model assessment) as standard abbreviations because they are well-known terms in the field of diabetes research.

Make sure the author uses abbreviations consistently after they have been defined and in accordance with the journal's guidelines. It is usually acceptable to redefine an abbreviation in the main text that has already been defined in the Abstract. Some journals ask their authors to redefine all abbreviations in the tables and figures while others consider the definition in the main text sufficient.

Abbreviations should be avoided in the main title of the paper so the reader can understand what the paper is about. The title is used to index the paper in literature databases and may not be recognised if it contains non-standard abbreviations. Some journals also ask that abbreviations not be defined in headings and subheadings but rather in the main text.

7 | Helping with the publication process

Publishing a scientific research paper involves more than writing the paper and submitting it. First, the author may wish to contact the journal Editor before submission to make sure their paper is suited to the scope of the journal. For this, they will need to write a pre-submission enquiry. Second, when they submit their paper, they have to explain why they think it should be published in their chosen journal. For this, they will need to write a cover letter. Finally, when they receive their comments from the peer reviewers, they may be invited to revise and resubmit their paper. For this, they will need to write a rebuttal letter.

In addition to needing help with their main manuscript, research authors may also ask you for help with pre-submission enquiries, cover letters and rebuttal letters. This chapter explains how to structure these letters.

Pre-submission enquiries

A pre-submission enquiry will not guarantee that the paper will be peer reviewed but it can avoid wasting time preparing a paper for submission to the wrong journal. When your client approaches you for help with their pre-submission enquiry, check that they are familiar with the journal's scope and that the journal in question accepts pre-submission enquiries. Your job will be to make sure the letter is easy to read and includes all the relevant information. Make sure the author has:

- followed the journal's instructions on preparing a pre-submission enquiry
- addressed the person responsible for dealing with submissions by name (if this information is provided on the journal's website)
- given the title of their manuscript and name of the journal in their

opening sentence (*We would like to enquire about the suitability of our manuscript entitled 'XXX' for publication in Clinical Oncology* is much better than *We would like to enquire about the suitability of our manuscript for publication in your journal*)
- told the journal Editor what they are attaching (the Abstract is usually sufficient to give an overview of the study but some journals may want to see the full manuscript)
- explained why they think their paper is suited to the journal (by describing their findings and what they bring to the field) and emphasised how these findings fit in with the journal's scope and why they will be interesting to the journal's readers
- thanked the journal Editor for their time and provided their contact details.

Cover letters

The cover letter accompanies the main manuscript when it is first submitted for publication. At the submission stage, research authors are often uninterested in the cover letter – they simply want to submit their paper after all those months of painstaking research! But they need to devote time and effort to writing this important letter. Journal Editors are not likely to send a manuscript out for peer review if the accompanying cover letter is badly written and full of errors. Encourage your client to take their time with the cover letter. Consider including it in your editing package – it could make all the difference to your client!

Here are some things to watch out for when editing the cover letter. Make sure the author has:

- followed the journal's instructions on writing a cover letter
- referred to the journal Editor by name
- given the title of the manuscript and the type of article in the opening sentence (*Please find attached our manuscript, entitled [manuscript title], which we would like to submit as a/an [type of article, such as original research article, case report, literature review] to [journal name]*)
- described the gap in the current knowledge that the study addresses and emphasised how these results will advance the field
- not exaggerated or made bold statements that are not supported

by their data (watch out for unnecessary intensifiers like *extremely* interesting or *very* significant)
- not copy and pasted text directly from the manuscript itself (encourage them to write new sentences with the journal's scope in mind)
- explained why their paper fits to the scope of the chosen journal and why their findings are relevant to the journal's readers
- suggested potential peer reviewers and explained why these people are suited to reviewing the paper (it is also acceptable to name peer reviewers who should not review the paper)
- included any statements required by the journal, such as conflicts of interest or confirmation that the manuscript has not been submitted for publication elsewhere
- thanked the journal Editor for their consideration.

Rebuttal letters

In the rebuttal letter, the author responds to the reviewers' comments and explains how any concerns have been addressed in their revised manuscript. Authors sometimes feel angry and resentful towards the reviewers, so make sure that the letter has a polite and respectful tone. It can help to remind them that peer review is a thankless job (the reviewers are not paid or acknowledged for their work) and that the comments and suggestions are intended to help improve the manuscript. Here are some points to watch out for in the rebuttal letter. Make sure the author has:

- followed the journal's instructions on writing the rebuttal letter
- addressed the journal Editor by name
- thanked the peer reviewers for their comments
- addressed each of the reviewers' comments in turn and has numbered their responses accordingly (it is useful to copy and paste the reviewers' comments into the letter and write the responses in a different colour underneath)
- explained any disagreements with the reviewers, with evidence to support their point
- guided the reviewers to changes in the text with page and line numbers.

8 | Resources

CIEP

Suggested courses

Medical Editing ciep.uk/training/choose-a-course/medical-editing

Plain English for Editors
ciep.uk/training/choose-a-course/plain-english-editors

Scientific style guides

American Institute of Physics (1997). *AIP Style Manual*. New York, NY: American Institute of Physics.
kmh-lanl.hansonhub.com/AIP_Style_4thed.pdf

American Mathematical Society (2021). *AMS Author Handbook*. Providence, RI: American Mathematical Society.
ams.org/arc/handbook/index.html

American Medical Association (2020). *AMA Manual of Style: A Guide for Authors and Editors*. New York, NY: Oxford University Press. (This is the style guide for the *JAMA* and *Archives* journals.)

American Psychological Association (2019). *Publication Manual of the American Psychological Association*. Washington, DC: American Psychological Association.

Banik, GM, Baysinger, G, Kamat, PV and Pienta, NJ (2020). *The ACS Guide to Scholarly Communication*. Washington, DC: American Chemical Society.

CSE Style Manual Committee (2014). *Scientific Style and Format: The CSE Manual for Authors, Editors, and Publishers*. Chicago, IL: The University of Chicago Press.

Institute of Electrical and Electronics Engineers (2016). *IEEE Editorial Style Manual*. Piscataway, NJ: IEEE. ieee.org/content/dam/ieee-org/ieee/web/org/conferences/style_references_manual.pdf

International Committee of Medical Journal Editors (2019). *Recommendations for the Conduct, Reporting, Editing, and Publication of Scholarly Work in Medical Journals*.
icmje.org/icmje-recommendations.pdf

Smart, P, Maisonneuve, H and Polderman, A (2013). *Science Editors' Handbook*. Redruth: EASE.

Non-scientific guides

CIEP Information Team (2020). *Being Aware of Gendered Language*. London: Chartered Institute of Editing and Proofreading.

CIEP Information Team (2021). *Easily Confused Words*. London: Chartered Institute of Editing and Proofreading.

Grey, S (2020). *The State of Gendered Language: What editors need to know in 2020*. London: Chartered Institute of Editing and Proofreading.

Higton, H (2020). *Academic Editing in the Humanities and Social Sciences*. London: Chartered Institute of Editing and Proofreading.

Hughes, G (2021). *Editing and Proofreading Numbers*. London: Chartered Institute of Editing and Proofreading.

Shakespeare, T (2021). *What's in a Name? Disability terminology for writers and editors*. London: Chartered Institute of Editing and Proofreading.

General information on scholarly publishing

Johnson, R, Watkinson, A and Mabe, M (2018). The STM Report: An overview of scientific and scholarly publishing. Oxford: International Association of Scientific, Technical and Medical Publishers.

Books on scientific writing

Graff, C and Birkenstein, C (2018). *"They Say I Say": The moves that matter in academic writing*. New York, NY: W. W. Norton & Company.

Greene, AE (2013). *Writing Science in Plain English*. Chicago, IL: The University of Chicago Press.

Hull, E (2018). *Health-related Scientific Articles in the 21st Century: Give readers nuggets!* Professional English.

Montgomery, SL (2017). *The Chicago Guide to Communicating Science*. Chicago, IL: The University of Chicago Press.

Schimel, J (2012). *Writing Science: How to write papers that get cited and proposals that get funded*. New York, NY: Oxford University Press.

Books on author editing

Matarese, V (2013). *Supporting Research Writing: Roles and challenges in multilingual settings*. Oxford: Chandos.

Matarese, V (2016). *Editing Research: The author editing approach to providing effective support to writers of research papers*. Medford, NJ: Information Today.

Plain English guides

Cutts, M (2020). *Oxford Guide to Plain English*. New York, NY: Oxford University Press.

Finley, L, Ripper, L and Carr, S (2019). *Editing into Plain English*. London: Chartered Institute of Editing and Proofreading.

Dehumanisation in clinical practice

Vaes, J (2013). Defensive dehumanization in the medical practice: A cross-sectional study from a health care worker's perspective. *British Journal of Social Psychology*, 52: 180–90.

Wayatz, A (2012). *A Patient, Not a Person*. Chicago, IL: Kellogg School of Management.
insight.kellogg.northwestern.edu/article/a_patient_not_a_person

Other useful resources

CONSORT website **consort-statement.org**

Medical editor Katharine O'Moore-Klopf's Copyeditors Knowledge Base **kokedit.com/ckb.php**

Paul Beverley's Macros for Editors **archivepub.co.uk/book.html**

Reporting guidelines of the EQUATOR (Enhancing the QUAlity and Transparency Of health Research) network **equator-network.org**

About the author

Dr Claire Bacon is a copyeditor and scientific language trainer based in Lippstadt, Germany. She edits pre-submission research papers and grant proposals for research scientists and post-submission research articles for Springer Nature. She also teaches courses on scientific writing for PhD students and other language professionals. She worked as a research scientist for 10 years before leaving academia in 2015 to train as a copyeditor. Passionate about clear communication in science, she is happier than ever helping scientists around the world get their important research ready for publication.

baconediting.com

Acknowledgements

My heartfelt thanks to Abi Saffrey, Cathy Tingle and Liz Dalby of the CIEP information team for their encouragement during the writing process and to copyeditor Sonia Cutler and reviewers Karen Digby, Emma Hoyle and Luke Finley for helping me to make this guide fit for purpose.

Claire Bacon

www.ingramcontent.com/pod-product-compliance
Lightning Source LLC
Chambersburg PA
CBHW071800080526
44588CB00013B/2312